Dearest Mom

_____

Heartfelt thanks for all the loving things you do and, most importantly, for who you are. May God bless you and keep you. May His favor shine upon you.

Love and Appreciation,

_____

_____

date

Numbers 6:24–25

Surprising Stories, Stirring Messages, and Refreshing Scriptures That Make the Heart Soar

heartlifters™

for Mom

LeAnn Weiss

messages by
Susan Duke

illustrated by
Katherine Cody
Kicklighter

HOWARD
PUBLISHING CO.

Our purpose at Howard Publishing is to:

- *Increase faith* in the hearts of growing
  Christians
- *Inspire holiness* in the lives of believers
- *Instill hope* in the hearts of struggling people
  everywhere

Because He's coming again!

Heartlifters™ for Mom © 2000 by LeAnn Weiss
All rights reserved. Printed in Hong Kong
Published by Howard Publishing Co., Inc.
3117 North 7th Street, West Monroe, Louisiana 71291-2227

00 01 02 03 04 05 06 07 08 09   10 9 8 7 6 5 4 3 2 1

Library of Congress Cataloging-in-Publication Data
Weiss, LeAnn.
    Heartlifters for mom : surprising stories, stirring messages, and refreshing scriptures that make the heart
soar / LeAnn Weiss ; messages by Susan Duke.
      p. cm.
    ISBN 1-58229-101-2
      1. Mothers—Religious life. 2. Motherhood—Religious aspects—Christianity. I. Duke, Susan. II. Title.

BV4529.18 .W45 2000
242'.6431—dc21

99-049940

Personalized scriptures by LeAnn Weiss, owner of Encouragement Company
3006 Brandywine Dr., Orlando, FL 32806; (407) 898-4410

Edited by Bob Kelly
Cover and interior design by LinDee Loveland
Illustrated by Katherine Cody Kicklighter

Contents

Nurturing CREATIVITY

There were lots of different words folks used to describe "Little Al," ranging from "retarded, addled, and troublesome" to "precocious, mischievous, and curious." Because he was frail at birth, with an abnormally large head, some feared he was defective. But his mother, Nancy Elliot, a devout Presbyterian, never gave up hope as she prayed for her seventh child.

It didn't take long for his mother to recognize there was nothing wrong with Al's mind. In fact, he was a precocious and inquisitive child, asking endless questions about everything. Once, his family became alarmed when they realized he'd been gone for hours. After a frantic search, they found him in the barn, calmly sitting on a makeshift nest in a straw box, trying to hatch eggs. "If the hens and gooses can do it," he wanted to know, "why can't I?"

Other early experiments had some serious consequences, causing the neighbors to label Al a troublemaker. At age six, he wanted to learn more about fire and decided his dad's barn would be a good place to start. Unfortunately, it was a breezy day and, in no time, Al's little fire became a roaring inferno, raging out of control. He barely got out alive, and the barn burned to the ground.

But even that narrow escape wasn't about to stop this curious little guy's voyage of discovery. He knew gas would inflate a balloon and decided he could do the same thing with a person. So he gave several doses of Seidlitz powder (a mild laxative) to a friend, believing it would generate enough gas to make him float through the air. Instead, his friend got quite sick and Al learned that, while Seidlitz powder didn't make people fly, it definitely put a ten-year-old "scientist" in the hot seat.

A hands-on learner, Al was bored by classroom routine, doodling and day-dreaming to wile away the hours. After only three months in school, he came home in tears, telling his mom that he'd overheard his teacher say his mind was "addled" and that staying in school would be a waste of time. But his mother knew better and went with Al to school the very next morning. Adamantly defending her bright son, she made her opinion of the teacher and school abundantly clear. Recognizing the potential of her son's vivid imagination, she primarily homeschooled Al after that painful incident.

His mother saw books as the best way to nurture his passionate curiosity, and she "implanted in his mind the love of learning." While Al never mastered spelling or math, he became a voracious reader, and a book she gave him helped him discover his passion for science.

Years later, Al reflected, "I was always a careless boy, and with a mother of different mental caliber I should have probably turned out badly. But her firmness, her sweetness, and her goodness were potent powers to keep me in the right path."

As a teenager, Al became an entrepreneur, selling candy and produce and publishing his own newspaper to help finance his experiments. No one wanted to buy his first patent, which was for an electric vote-recording machine.

Al's first significant invention, an improved stock ticker machine, sold for forty thousand dollars. His invention of the kinescope, a motion picture camera, paved the way for the movie industry. Although virtually deaf from the age of twelve, his favorite invention was the phonograph.

His mother, Nancy Elliot Edison, died before he reached the pinnacle of success. Little did she realize that her son's lifelong drive to find solutions to problems would usher in a new age of technology, with more than a thousand patents issued in his name. But Thomas Alva Edison, better known as the creator of the incandescent light bulb, never forgot her contributions to his many achievements. "My mother was the making of me," he would say. "She understood me; she let me follow my bent. She cast over me an influence which has lasted all my life."

Nurturing

When you hear the word creativity, do you think of great artists, old masters whose priceless masterpieces grace the halls of museums and galleries? Maybe you think of architects who sit for countless hours designing buildings that will astound all who view their magnificent structure—or sculptors who start with an idea and sculpt it into art with detailed precision.

Or...as a mom, your first thoughts just might be of the crayon-colored scene drawn on construction paper that graces your refrigerator door. Not exactly the art of an old master, but genius, perhaps, just the same! Examine it closely and you'll see much more than colors and paper and shapes. You'll see imagination personified. You'll see a wishing heart, a fleeting dream, and even faith. You see, faith is part of creating—believing with wide-eyed wonder that you have the capability of taking an idea or a thought and giving it life. It's all there—in the details. In the yellow sun, the brown-and gold-colored road, the black V-shaped wings of soaring birds, and the multicolored rainbow.

We are all born with creativity. And it's been said that of all human beings, children possess the strongest inherent creative abilities. So to a child, creativity is as natural as breathing or blinking. And as mothers, we are given the unequaled privilege of nurturing, guiding, and igniting our children's creative potential. Acknowledging their uniqueness and teaching children to embrace and explore their creative

Nurturing

interests give them wings not only to be who they are today, but also what they can become tomorrow.

God, the Father of all creativity, loves to nurture creativity in His children. That's why He gives mothers the creative keys to inspire, teach, unlock, and awaken the joy of expression in our own children.

Just as our lives are the empty canvases on which God the Master Artist paints, our children's lives are shaped by our loving touches. You never know what your nurturing brush strokes of love and encouragement may someday produce. But one thing is certain…it will be a "work of heart"!

six

You are uniquely designed for My eternal purposes . . .

Availing PRAYER

For a teenager who couldn't read music and had no formal training, the dream of one day leading a large choir seemed an improbable one. But Carol Hutchins had a song in her heart to accompany her dream, and she had a love for music inherited from her pianist grandmother and her father, an opera singer turned pastor.

It was at her dad's church that Carol first met Jim, the young man who, in 1969, became her husband. After their marriage, Carol's dad persuaded Jim, who had no seminary training or experience, to try his hand at pastoring. Carol's dad steered them toward an inner-city church that had been birthed through the prayers of Carol's mom—a church that would one day touch many people for the glory of God.

When Jim and Carol answered the call to this struggling church, which had fewer than twenty members and less than ten dollars in the bank, it was on the verge of closing. Then, one morning, Jim abruptly stopped his sermon and called his tiny congregation together for prayer. It was a major breakthrough, the first of many. They found that God is drawn to those who humbly and honestly admit how much they need Him. Prayer became the barometer of their ministry.

Despite her lack of formal training, Carol was a gifted organist and pianist and took the first step toward realizing her dream. Starting with just nine people who were as untrained as she, her choir began to take shape. Carol had learned that life in music comes through prayer, and her choir practices always began with a half-hour of prayer time and often involved more prayer and worship than actual practice—and sometimes no practice at all.

From that modest beginning, her choir grew into a large and highly skilled ensemble that recorded several albums and held outreach concerts for packed audiences at New York's world-famous Radio City Music Hall.

Despite such success, Carol wanted to get her kids out of the inner-city atmosphere. Their eldest daughter, Chrissy, who'd always been a model child, began to stray from her parents and from God. As Chrissy's rebellion escalated, Carol endured many sleepless nights, not knowing where her precious child might be.

In the midst of a growing ministry, the enemy taunted Carol's mind with dark thoughts: *Carol, you and your husband can go ahead to reach the world for Christ—but I'll have your children. I've already got the first one. I'm coming for the next two.*

Carol turned to her piano for comfort, and God gave her a song about His faithfulness that has probably touched more people than any other song she has written. Carol and Jim continued to press on with prayer, but Chrissy's rebellion grew and, eventually, she left home.

One night, during the weekly church prayer meeting, someone felt deeply burdened for Chrissy, and the entire church stopped to intercede for her. Less than two days later, a sobbing Chrissy was on her knees in her family's kitchen, asking for her parents' and God's forgiveness. The prodigal had come home!

After more than twenty years, Carol Cymbala continues to direct the Grammy Award–winning, 240-voice Brooklyn Tabernacle Choir. A melting pot of people representing the full economic spectrum, including business and professional men and women, street people, former prostitutes, and drug addicts, the multiracial choir and its spin-off have won a Dove Award and many other nominations.

"I just want to see people drawn to Jesus Christ," Carol says. "I want the music to be the arrow that points them to Him."

Carol is even more joyful now that Chrissy has moved back to the area and helps her in leading the choir. Chrissy's husband is an assistant pastor at the church, which has grown to more than six thousand in number.

Carol Cymbala testifies that persistent calling upon the Lord breaks through every stronghold of the devil, for with God nothing is impossible.

PRAYER

waiting

Have you ever sat in the dark after a power outage from a severe storm? You don't move about quite as freely as you normally would. You light candles…and wait. And then, when the power suddenly comes back on, you breathe a sigh a relief. You have power again—and you can run your dishwasher, stereo, computer, or washing machine.

There may be tumultuous storms that bring darkness into your life. Circumstances may catch you off guard and cause you to lose your footing temporarily. But unlike the electric company, you have a power source that will never leave you in the dark!

Prayer is the lamp that keeps you company in dim and despairing moments. It's an instant connection between your heart and God's. And He has promised to never leave you comfortless. Prayer is your acknowledgment of total dependency on the one and only true source of power. And for mothers, it is an understanding that in your times of weakness, He is ever watchful—ever strong.

While some prayers are answered instantly, others require times of waiting. But while you're waiting, His light burns brightly within your heart, keeping vigil until the answer comes.

thirteen

Awaiting

Prayer is not a spare tire, an SOS call for help, or a fire escape. Prayer is an abiding and fervent trust in a God who is moved with compassion on our behalf.

When you pray you can rest, believing Jesus is ever interceding for you. You can be confident as a mom, knowing you have a direct connection to the Throne of Grace. Small conflicts and great battles are fought through the power lines of prayer. And no power outage shall come upon your heart's dwelling! Turn out the lights…God is awake!

Your prayers are powerful and effective...

Loving UNCONDITIONALLY

Singer-actress Frances Octavia Smith always dreamed of raising a large family. She'd had one child, now grown, and her dream was fading. Then, at age thirty-five, she married a widowed movie star and saw her dream reborn. On her wedding day, she slipped into a closet and prayed: "Dear God, you know the great responsibility of marrying this man with three motherless children. Please help me. Give me courage and the understanding to establish a Christian home like the one I had as a child."

Less than two years later, Frances was elated to discover she was pregnant. She'd been told that without extensive surgery her childbearing days were over, and she considered her surprise pregnancy a miracle.

On August 26, 1950, the long-awaited day came and their "Little Angel," Robin Elizabeth, was born. An anxious and groggy Frances was overjoyed when her husband whispered, "Honey, she's beautiful; she has little ears just like yours."

But her joy was short-lived. Days later, she learned that Robin wasn't responding to routine tests. Her heart sank when the doctors told her the baby was "Mongoloid." Joined by her supportive husband, she had many questions and tears. "I had wanted a little girl to be proud of and to show off as every mother does. After all, I had to keep up my image of success," she remembered. "But God sent me a little girl society was not proud of to teach me humility."

Their doctor counseled, "Love will help more than anything else in a situation like this—more than all the hospitals and medical science in the world." So, they took Robin into their home and hearts.

More bad news followed. Doctors found the baby had a serious congenital heart defect and urged her celebrity parents to put her in an institution before they became too attached. Even though Robin wasn't a "normal" baby, her parents couldn't imagine such a thing. Despite predictions that Robin wouldn't live long, they replied, "No! We'll keep her and do all we can for her."

Eager to find a cure for her baby, Frances went to numerous specialists to learn all she could about Down's syndrome. Countless dead-end hopes and astronomical medical expenses seemed insignificant compared to her growing love for Robin.

Then, just days before she was two, Robin succumbed to a ravaging fever and entered the presence of the Lord. What had been planned as a party was tearfully changed to a funeral, and the "Little Angel" was laid to rest on her second birthday.

Overcome with grief, Frances wrote a love epistle about the blessings of Robin's handicapped life. At the time, because of the stigma, Down's syndrome children were seldom, if ever, seen in public. Parents across the country responded, sharing how Robin's story gave them new hope to love their own special-needs children instead of hiding them in institutions.

While no one could replace Robin, Frances shares, "Every time I see a Down's syndrome child at work in school, sheltered workshops, or in routine jobs offered in many organizations, I can almost see Robin's beautiful, beautiful smile."

Frances later became the mother of four other children through adoption and foster care. With nine children in all, her dream of raising a large family had come true and, in 1957, she was honored as "California Mother of the Year."

Professionally known as Dale Evans Rogers, "Queen of the West," her world-renowned career included twenty-seven movies as costar with her late husband, Roy Rogers, "King of the Cowboys." Together they also produced *The Roy Rogers Show*, which ran on television until 1957. Dale's love tribute to Robin, *Angel Unaware*, is still in print and has touched more than two million lives.

UNCONDITIONALLY

Loving

When you became a mom, you were given a unique and special gift. It wasn't wrapped in a box covered with pretty paper or tied with blue or pink ribbon. But it came special delivery, straight from heaven and placed at your heart's door. And when you opened the door and unwrapped the unexpected gift, you knew immediately that whatever the years of childrearing might bring, because of this special gift, you would be equipped with everything you'd ever need to be the best mom you could possibly be.

The gift? Unconditional love. Not the kind of love that measures what is given in return, but the kind of selfless love that gives without reserve—endlessly, tirelessly, without doubts or judgment. Unconditional love comes wrapped in grace and tied with ribbons of acceptance, unmerited favor, and devotion. It's an eternal gift that is with you every single moment of motherhood. It changes your perspective and allows you to see the world with new vision. It's a tempering of old attitudes, and it's new light in dark moments. It motivates, energizes, pursues, soothes and heals, dares to hope, and swims against tides of unbelief.

Isn't it wonderful to know that the love that allows us to wipe spilled milk, clean dirty faces, and always believe the best is the same love bestowed upon us by a loving heavenly Father? It's the kind of love that looks beyond the way things might appear, beyond society's labels, beyond reasoning or logic, and beyond mistakes.

UNCONDITIONALLY

There are many qualities of unconditional love. But the most miraculous of all is that it was given to you. You possess it, you hold it tightly in your heart, and yet you give it away time and time again. Unconditional love is truly a gift that keeps on giving.

Experience the fullness of My eternal love…

Let your life be clean and true
before God, and it will be the first
sharp tool God uses in marking
your child for him.

—Anne Gimenez

Encouraging CHARACTER

Jobs were scarce in 1932 when a young man called Dutch graduated from college. The nation was in the depths of the Great Depression, with unemployment at a staggering 26 percent. Dutch looked far and wide for work, but without success. Tired, defeated in spirit, and nearly penniless, he wound up thumbing a ride back home. Learning of an opening at a local Montgomery Ward store, he quickly applied and was crushed when someone else was hired.

Although his close-knit family was considered poor, his parents, Jack and Nellie, always provided enough to eat and plenty of love. Dutch grew up observing how love, common sense, and purpose unite families, helping them overcome great adversities. His mother assumed the spiritual responsibilities, starting with regular Sunday school and morning church attendance.

Nellie's great religious faith rubbed off on her son. A good-hearted woman who always looked for and found the best in people, she would frequently reach out to prisoners at the local jail by taking them hot meals. She reminded Dutch and his brother to "treat your neighbor as you would want your neighbor to treat you" and to "judge everyone by how they act, not what they are." In her eyes, there was no more grievous sin than a racial slur or religious or racial intolerance.

Nellie taught Dutch the value of prayer as well as how to dream and to believe he could make his dreams come true through hard work. She taught him that God had a plan for everyone. She believed that seemingly random "twists of fate" were really orchestrated parts of God's divine plan.

Although his parents never completed grade school, they encouraged Dutch to better himself. He paid his own way through college, aided by a Needy Student Scholarship, and was elected Student Council and Booster Club president. But graduation brought little reason to celebrate. By then, millions were out of work, overwhelmed with crushing debts.

When Dutch returned home after his fruitless job search, Nellie tenderly reminded him that all things, even disheartening setbacks, are part of God's plan. She encouraged him with the assurance that one day he would look back and find himself thinking, *If I hadn't had that problem back then, then this better thing that did happen wouldn't have happened to me.*

Dutch recalled, "I left home again in search of work. Although I didn't know it then, I was beginning a journey that would...fulfill all of my dreams and then some. My mother, as usual, was right." Years later, he wrote, "To our mothers we owe our highest esteem, for it is from their gift of life that the flow of events begins that shapes our destiny. A mother's love, nurturing, and beliefs are among the strongest influences molding the development and character of our youngsters."

On Mother's Day, 1985, in a radio address, Dutch said, "I find my thoughts turning to my own mother.... She was truly a remarkable woman—ever so strong in her determination, yet always tender, always giving of herself to others. She never found time in her life to complain; she was too busy living those values she sought to impart in my brother and myself. She was the greatest influence on my life, and as I think of her this weekend, I remember the words of Lincoln, 'All that I am, or hope to be, I owe to my mother.'"

Just as his mother had assured him when he was at his lowest point, God did have a better plan for him. Dutch found a job as a sports announcer before moving to Hollywood and becoming a film star. In 1966, he was elected governor of California, winning reelection to a second term in 1970. In 1981, he became the fortieth president of the United States, holding the nation's highest office for eight years.

"If I'd gotten the job I wanted at Montgomery Ward, I suppose I would never have left Illinois," reflected Ronald Wilson Reagan.

CHARACTER

Encouraging

You may not realize it, but your children watch everything you do, hear everything you say, and mimic your actions and attitudes. That's how they learn. You could call it "growing character." And the kind of soil and environment in which seeds of character are grown will determine the kind of harvest you produce.

It's true that children learn what they live. Teaching good habits is a fairly easy task, but character is developed and instilled over many years. No one is automatically born with character. As a mother, encouraging and mentoring character in your children while they are in your care is one of the single most important assignments you'll ever be given.

When you exhibit patience, a seed of patience is planted in the pliable heart of your child. When you do your best to right an injustice or make a stand for fairness, a silent witness is listening with trusting little ears. When you choose honesty over dishonesty; when you stand courageous through great trials; when you persevere through pressures and obstacles— or take the time to nourish friendships, you've mentored a precious and eager student of character.

Encouraging your children to always do their best, hold fast to their dreams, and behold the hands of God in which their lives are held will sustain them for a lifetime. Someday, it will not be the material wealth your children possess that

Encouraging

expresses their worth, but the kind of person they've become. To have been encouraged with a heritage of character by a loving mom will equip and empower them for loyalty, giving them a priceless legacy to pass down to their own children.

Someone once said, "Character is what angels say about you before the throne of God." And you, dear mom, are giving the angels plenty of good things to talk about!

Look to Me for comfort and encouragement…

If God, like a father, denies us what we want now, it is in order to give us some far better thing later on. The will of God, we can rest assured, is invariably a better thing.

—Elisabeth Elliot

Trusting GOD

When three-year-old Amy, the first of David and Catherine's seven children, awoke one morning and ran to the mirror, she was very disappointed to see the same old brown eyes staring back at her. After all, her mother had taught her that Jesus hears and answers our prayers, so the night before, she'd confidently asked Him for blue eyes, just like her mom's. Catherine tenderly explained that sometimes God answers our prayers "No" or "Wait" because He knows what is best for us.

Years later, when Amy was a grown woman, Catherine received a letter from her, dated January 14, 1892. "My precious Mother," the letter read, "Have you ever given your child unreservedly to the Lord for whatever He wills?... Oh, may He strengthen you to say yes to Him if He asks something which costs."

Motherly pride filled Catherine's heart as she read of Amy's passion for God and for those who had never heard of Jesus. Amy's letter told of her desire to go to the mission field. But she also gave several reasons for not going, including the desire to stay near her widowed mother and family. At the end of her letter, however, she wrote, "Yesterday...I went to my room and just asked the Lord what it all meant, what did He wish me to do, and, Mother, as clearly as I ever heard you speak, I heard him say 'GO YE.'"

Victorian stories of the time romanticized missionary life, but Catherine realized the sacrifices and dangers her daughter would face far away from their lovely Irish countryside. Before her father's death, Amy and her family had been used to having more than enough financially—even for boarding school and a governess. It would be much different on the mission field.

Would Amy be lonely? Transportation was slow. Letters and prayers would be their only link. And what about marriage? How would Amy adjust to the meager economic conditions of missionary life? Would she catch a disease from poor sanitation or lack of proper medical treatment?

She wanted badly to hold on to Amy, but Catherine knew she must release her daughter to follow God's will. She wrote back, "Darling, when He asks you now to go away from my reach, can I say nay? No, no, Amy; He is yours—you are His—to take you where He pleases and to use you as He pleases. I can trust you to Him, and I do."

After short terms in Japan and Sri Lanka, Amy settled in India, where she grew to appreciate her God-given brown eyes. Dressed in her native sari, those eyes helped Amy blend in with Indian women, gaining her entrance into forbidden Hindu temples.

When she learned that babies were dedicated to the temple and wed as young as five to temple priests, Amy was horrified. With the help of coworkers, she established the Dohnavur Fellowship, a unique ministry that rescued children and provided them with a safe and healthy Christ-centered home.

In 1905, her mother had the privilege of visiting India and seeing the fruit of Amy's ministry in the home where she was raising rescued children, teaching them to love Jesus. With grandmotherly affection, Catherine embraced Amy's ever-growing family.

Amy believed in a life of consecration to God, noting, "The saddest thing one meets is the nominal Christian." Although she never married, Amy devoted her life to almost nine hundred children during her fifty-six years of evangelism in India. Those who knew her affectionately called her "Amma," which means mother. She wrote thirty-five books about her experiences and became a role model to many future Christian leaders, including Elisabeth Elliot and Ruth Bell Graham.

Amy Carmichael often prayed, "Holy Spirit, think through me till Your ideas are my ideas." Her obedience to God's will helped make His love known, especially to the people of India. During one period of immense trials she wrote, "To will what God wills brings peace."

Remember how you felt when you first held your baby's chubby little hand? All the preparation in the world couldn't have readied you for that moment! Holy, sweet, and silent, with that first touch, an eternal bond began. Emotions flooded your heart. Thoughts you never could have even imagined before that hour whirled like a top, spinning endlessly through your head.

You were holding a miracle! And as you beheld that tiny miracle, dreams danced in your heart. Suddenly, you realized the awesome responsibility that was yours. That child—that bundle of pure innocent love—would be depending on you for every need—physical, emotional, and spiritual—from then on! And between the folds of excitement and silent benediction, you knew your life would be forever changed by the chubby little hand you were holding.

I wonder…did Mary feel the same desires and responsibility to be the best guardian over her precious son as she held him close that first Bethlehem night? Did she suddenly feel inadequate to provide, teach, and protect this precious gift of life? She had only one choice—to trust God.

God gives mothers natural instincts for raising children. But He also gives spiritual wisdom. In those first reverent moments—knowing that when you look at your child, you're looking at God's child—you recognize the gift He's entrusted to your care.

thirty-seven

Trusting

God gives mothers the kind of wisdom that transcends the desire to be a great mom. It's wisdom that depends on the only One who could possibly love your child more than you do.

Deep within your heart, if you'll listen, you just might hear a lullaby—God singing to you, His child, about trusting Him, His love, His will, and His guidance. It's a sonnet of peace that assures you as a mom…while you are rocking the cradle, He is rocking the world!

I will keep you and yours in My perfect peace....

Instilling COMMITMENT

When she was born hydrocephalic, with fluid backed up around her brain, her future seemed uncertain. But the steadfast faith of her mother and father, joined by the believers in their church, was instrumental in seeing her through a dangerous surgery. Miraculously, she didn't need a shunt installed in her brain like many "waterhead" babies require and suffered no brain damage.

Her family tree included five generations of pastors, teachers, and singers. "I don't remember a time that I didn't love the Lord. It was easy to fall in love and commit to Christ. I watched my parents," she reflected.

Her mother, a dedicated pastor's wife, recognized her daughter's natural musical ability. Although the young girl played primarily by ear, her mother insisted on adding piano lessons. By age nine, the same year she personally invited Jesus into her heart, she was the full-time church pianist at their 350-member church in the inner city of Jackson, Michigan.

Growing up, she sometimes felt burdened by her responsibility as pianist and choir director. But her mother wouldn't allow her to quit or to slack off in her duties or lessons. She learned the value of commitment and discipline from watching her mother. "I don't ever remember my mom giving up on a person or a project," she recalled. "Mom always gives 110 percent to whatever she does, serving God with both her hands and heart."

In 1984, her hard work began paying off. She entered a songwriting and vocal competition at Christian Artists Music Seminar in the Rockies and ranked as a finalist. After learning that songwriting is a craft, requiring both inspiration and perspiration, she went home, applied the techniques she'd learned, and wrote the award-winning classic "All Rise." When she returned the following year, she took the limelight, winning both the vocal and songwriting competitions. Soon people were calling her to sing and to write songs. In 1989, Word Records recruited her for her first professional album.

She vividly remembers the time after her father's death when her mother asked how she was doing. Still grieving, she replied, "I'm hanging in there." Her mother painted a word picture she'll never forget. She responded, "My dear, you could just hang in there, but is that what you really want? When you are 'hanging,' you are exposed like a sheet on your grandmother's clothesline. You have loose ends and freely dangle as the wind blows." Her mom continued, "Instead, as children of God, we are called to follow Ephesians 6 by standing firm." She heeded her mother's exhortation, noting, "I've never used that phrase again. Now when people ask how I'm doing, I purposely say 'I'm standing.' I'm no longer content to settle for less."

As her musical career has progressed, she has graced the stage with Bill and Gloria Gaither, presidents Jimmy Carter and George Bush, and preachers such as Dr. Billy Graham. Babbie Mason has recorded thirteen albums, written more than five hundred songs, and has received two Dove Awards. Her powerful lyrics and melodies have made her songs some of the best loved by choirs and soloists around the world. On her *Heritage in Faith* CD, Babbie especially enjoyed singing a duet with her mother titled "Stop by the Church," which won a Dove Award.

As a mother of two, Babbie notes, "I'm realizing more and more that godly heritage is a gift." Her children, Jerry and Chaz, both gifted musicians, are involved in her ministry. As she and husband, Charles, raise their two sons, she is trying to instill the same kind of commitment in them that her mother demonstrated to her. For nearly forty years, her mom, Georgie, faithfully served at the side of her husband, Reverend George Wade, at a church they built from the ground up. "Mom had such an unmovable commitment to help me fulfill God's destiny. I want my sons to stand in Christ with that same commitment."

Instilling

Have you ever watched a mama bird in the spring as she builds a nest, hatches her babies, and feeds them one by one? If you have, then you've observed commitment firsthand. She commits herself to caring for her young, sheltering them with her wings when the rains come, and then gently pushing them from their cozy nest when it's time to teach them to fly. When one falls to the ground, she swoops down to her waiting fledgling, urging it onward and upward once more. She never lets them give up. They may only flap their wings gently at first, while half-hopping, half-flying from limb to limb. But after falling several times to the ground and being coaxed by mama to try again, they at last soar gracefully from their comfortable nest. And so a new cycle of life begins.

Mothers have the inherent ability to teach and instill knowledge and character. You teach how to tie shoelaces, speak words, and use a spoon. But all the while, as your children experience your commitment to them, seeds of great significance are being planted in their little spirits—seeds that grow as they grow and establish core values that will stand through life's testings.

Christ exemplified His commitment to us when He came to earth, lived as a man, never gave up on fulfilling His mission, and endured the cross for our sakes. And although He could have called ten thousand angels to stop His suffering or decided in Gethsemane's garden to let the cup

Instilling

of pain He knew He must drink pass from Him, He didn't. He proved that commitment is giving yourself fully to something you believe in or love.

When you instill commitment in your children, you prepare them to valiantly face disappointments, setbacks, and difficult trials with a determined heart. You teach them to never give up on their dreams, always hope in tomorrow, and soar beyond every cloud of disillusionment in search of sunshine.

Moms can learn a valuable lesson from mama bird's simple philosophy that befits our children as well. "If at first you don't succeed, stick with it, keep focused, and fly, fly again!" For, just beyond the treetops—just beyond the sun-split clouds is commitment's reward.

Don't lose heart in doing good…

Serving JOYFULLY

Hers was a fairly typical middle-class home, with little to indicate what the future held for little Agnes. The youngest of three children, she lived with her parents and siblings in a large, comfortable home. "We lived for each other and made every effort to make one another happy," Agnes reflected.

Agnes's mother, Drana Bernai, devoted herself to helping others. She never let any of the poor people who knocked on their door leave hungry or empty-handed. Agnes often accompanied her mother when Drana routinely distributed food and clothing to the poor. She paid close attention to her mother's tender care of others, without heed to their disheveled appearance and often-foul odor.

At first, Agnes just watched. But before long, she was helping her mother clean and bandage wounds, administer smiles, and listen to the lonely. Drana would smile and whisper to her daughter, "When you help people like this, it's just like helping Jesus." She never drew attention to their deeds.

At twelve, Agnes felt God was calling her to a vocation to help the poor. Hesitant to leave her family, Agnes pondered her future and waited. When she was eighteen, she decided she was ready to venture out. With Drana's blessing, Agnes left the comforts of her home to serve the poor, never realizing it was the last time she would ever see her mother or sister.

Eventually, Agnes felt led to move into the slums of one of the poorest cities in the world to live among and serve the "poorest of poor." Her legacy went far beyond social work. Whether cheerfully scrubbing a dirty toilet or holding the hand of a dying AIDS patient, she dedicated herself to doing ordinary things with extraordinary love.

Agnes showed her coworkers how to give the gift of human dignity to people who previously had nothing or felt that no one cared. It was her firm belief that "it's not how much we do, but how much love we put in the doing."

In 1950, she founded the Missionaries of Charity. Shunning regular funding from the government, relying solely on donations, Agnes and her twelve initial coworkers started schools for children, homes for the dying, orphanages, and hospitals for lepers and mental patients. Special homes were also established for alcoholics, drug addicts, AIDS patients, abused women and children, and other neglected people.

"We are committed to feed Christ who is hungry, committed to clothe Christ who is naked, committed to take in Christ who has no home—and to do all this with a smile on our face and bursting with joy," Agnes emphasized.

In 1979, she was awarded the Nobel Peace Prize, accepting it "in the name of the hungry, the naked, the homeless…and those who feel unwanted, uncared for." She earmarked the $190,000 award to build another leper colony and homes for the poor.

Dressed in her trademark sari and sandals, Agnes was honored by presidents, leaders, and royalty throughout the world. Instead of seeking personal gain, she used her popularity to educate the public on the plight of the poor and to encourage others to become involved.

"Begin at home by saying something good to your child, to your husband…. Begin by helping someone in need in your community, at work, or at school. Begin by making whatever you do something beautiful for God," was her simple call to action.

On September 5, 1997, Agnes, much better known by her religious name, Mother Teresa of Calcutta, died at the age of eighty-seven. One of the most respected women in the world, her funeral drew more than twelve thousand people, including many world dignitaries. Millions watched on television, mourning the passing of the petite, wrinkled-faced woman who had humbly served her way to greatness.

Mother Teresa once said something that perhaps best described her remarkable life of service: "In our action, we are instruments in God's hand, and He writes beautifully."

Serving

JOYFULLY

Have you heard the phrase "If mama ain't happy, ain't nobody happy?" Well, truer words were never spoken! But not in the context you might at first think. You may interpret this phrase to mean that mama will make life miserable for everyone else if she's not happy! But perhaps there's a deeper message behind these words.

Do you realize that you, as a mom, have the privilege of creating a warm and loving atmosphere for your family? Only you can give your home those special warm touches that truly make a house a home. Your home reflects who you are, what you feel, and what you want others to feel when they come in.

The curtains on the windows, the fresh flowers on the table, the candle you light during dinner, the delightful smells of apple pie or your special pot roast say to your family or visiting friends, "I care. And all the things I do are my way of showing how much you mean to me."

Every little act of kindness, concern, and preparation has a ripple effect...much like the stone skipped on water. God has given you the creativity, responsibility, and desire to help and serve others. And when you joyfully embrace your God-given role, that same joy spreads to everyone around you.

As you serve others daily through your gift of hospitality, may you be reminded to also be aware of every attached blessing. For there would be no dirty dishes without the pro-vision of good food, no laundry without the blessing of nice clothes, and no dirty bathrooms to clean without modern

fifty-three

Serving JOYFULLY

conveniences. There are many in this world who have no shoes to pick up or beds to sleep in and make up the next morning.

Serving others is no easy task, and you probably wonder sometimes if anyone really appreciates or notices all you do. But you can believe, although you may not often hear the words, that they do.

And even more—God cares that you are cheerfully and thankfully fulfilling a calling only a mom has the opportunity to respond to! You not only create blessings for others, you are a blessing! So, I guess you might say, "If Mama's happy, everybody's happy!"

What you do for others honors Me...

Every child has been
created for a greater thing—
to love and be loved.

—MOTHER TERESA

Sources

More than one hundred sources were used in compiling the biographical sketches in this book. The following sources were primary.

Thomas Alva Edison

Baldwin, Neil. *Edison: Inventing the Century.* New York: Hyperion, 1995.

Edison, Thomas Alva. *The Diary and Sundry Observations of Thomas Alva Edison.* New York: Greenwood Press Publishers, 1948 (reprinted 1968).

Josephson, Matthew. *Edison: A Biography.* New York: John Wiley & Sons, 1959, 1992.

Carol Cymbala

Brooklyn Tabernacle Choir Records

Cymbala, Jim and Dean Merrill. *Fresh Wind, Fresh Fire.* Grand Rapids, Mich.: Zondervan Publishing, 1997.

Dale Evans Rogers

Evans, Dale. *In the Hands of the Potter.* Nashville, Tenn.: Thomas Nelson Publishers, 1994.

Rogers, Dale Evans. *Angel Unaware.* Grand Rapids, Mich.: Flemming H. Revell, 1953, 1981.

Sources

Rogers, Dale Evans. *My Personal Picture Album*. Old Tappan, N. J.: Fleming H. Revell, 1971.

Rogers, Roy with Carlton Stowers. *Happy Trails: The Story of Roy Rogers and Dale Evans*. Waco, Tex.: Word Books, 1979.

Ronald Reagan

Reagan, Ronald. *An American Life: The Autobiography*. New York: Simon & Schuster, 1990.

President Reagan's Mother's Day Proclamation, April 6, 1983.

President Reagan's May 11, 1985, Radio Address to the Nation.

Amy Carmichael

Dick, Lois Hoadley. *Let the Little Children Come*. Chicago, Ill.: Moody Press, 1984.

Elliot, Elisabeth. *A Chance to Die*. Grand Rapids, Mich.: Fleming H. Revell, 1987.

Wellman, Sam. *Amy Carmichael: A Life Abandoned to God*. Uhrichsville, Ohio: Barbour House Publishing, 1998.

White, Kathleen. *Amy Carmichael*. Minneapolis, Minn.: Bethany House, 1986.

Sources

Babbie Mason

Mason, Babbie. *Heritage of Faith*. Nashville, Tenn.:
    Word Records, 1996.
Personal Interview with Babbie Mason on August 8, 1999.
Babbie's musical tapes and CDs are available through Christian bookstores.

Mother Teresa

Mother Teresa. *Mother Teresa: In My Own Words*. New York: Gramercy Books, 1996.
Mother Teresa, edited by José Luis Gonzalez-Balado. *Loving Jesus*. Ann Arbor, Mich.:
    Servant Publications, 1991.
Mother Teresa. *Words to Love By*. Notre Dame, Ind.: Ave Maria Press, 1993.
Wellman, Sam. *Mother Teresa: Mission of Charity*. Uhrichsville, Ohio: Barbour
    Publishing, 1997.

Other books that include LeAnn Weiss's paraphrased Scriptures:

Hugs for Dad
Hugs for Grandparents
Hugs for the Holidays
Hugs for the Hurting
Hugs for Kids
Hugs for Mom
Hugs for Sisters
Hugs for Teachers
Hugs for Those in Love
Hugs for Women
Hugs to Encourage and Inspire
Hugs from Heaven: Embraced by the Savior
Hugs from Heaven: On Angel Wings
Hugs from Heaven: The Christmas Story

Also by LeAnn Weiss:

Hugs for Friends
Heartlifters™ for Friends
Heartlifters™ for Hope and Joy
Heartlifters™ for Women